C000098038

THE
COMMON THREAD
THAT BINDS US

THE WISDOM OF
DIVERSITY AND INCLUSION

by

Kenneth Little Hawk
and Beverly Miller

ETERNAL WAYS

i

ETERNAL WAYS

Published by Eternal Ways

For further information on Kenneth Little Hawk and Beverly Miller, visit the
following websites:

www.WisdomOfDiversity.com
www.KennethLittleHawk.com
www.GoodHeartTribe.com

For further information on Eternal Ways visit www.EternalWays.com

Published by Eternal Ways, Massachusetts, USA
Printed in the United States of America
First Printing: October 2011

ISBN 10 0615548164
ISBN 13 9780615548166

www.WisdomOfDiversity.com

"You are a national treasure."

Naomi C. Earp, Chairwoman (2006-2009), E.E.O.C
(U.S. Equal Employment Opportunity Commission)

WHO IS LITTLE HAWK?

Little Hawk is an internationally reknowned inspirational speaker. Being Mi'kmaq and Mohawk, he is able to illustrate how Native American culture broadens the Diversity and Inclusion topic to encompass not only the choices we make to live in harmony with one another, but the choices we must make to live in harmony with our environment.

For Native Americans, storytelling is an important tool for teaching responsibility, respect, and how to live in a good way. Little Hawk's stories teach that most of life's challenges can be overcome and that we need to share our good-heartedness with all people because we are ALL related.

All the Little Hawk stories and live performances have been co-created and co-produced by Little Hawk and his wife, Beverly Miller. As a creative team that has successfully worked together for over 30 years, Beverly and Little Hawk have produced hundreds of inspiring shows for corporations, museums, schools, and the federal government: A total of more than three million people all over the world.

www.KennethLittleHawk.com

Little Hawk teaches about the importance of laughter.
Still photo from the REAWAKEN movie. Watch it at ReawakenMovie.com.

CONTENTS

WHO IS LITTLE HAWK? v

CONTENTS vii

FOREWORD

Multicultural Inclusion: The Thread That Binds............................1

INTRODUCTION

Diversity Lessons of First Nations People 5

SECTION 1: In The Words of Little Hawk 7

The Medicine Wheel 9

We Are All Related 11

Let the Winds Blow..13

Where We Used to Run and Play 15

The Seventh Generation 19

Sweet Smell of Peace 21

The Birds' Song..23

The Indian on the Ledge..25

Sunrise on the Mountaintop 27

The Eagle Feather 29

After the Rain 31

The Gift 33

Quotes from Little Hawk 35

SECTION 2: Little Hawk's Stories of Respect and Compassion 55

Elder at the Gathering..57

Two Wolves 59

The Talking Tree 61

The Birds had a Contest 65

Good-Heart Tribe 69

Thank You, Grandfather 77

SECTION 3: Native American Wisdom 79

Words of Peace 81

Sacred Way Prayer 83

Equal Justice 85

A Traditional Chinook Blessing 87

Sitting Bull 89

Elders Circle 91

John Fire Lame Deer 93

Wallace Black Elk 95

Mourning Dove 97

Oren Lyons, Jr. 99

Nuxalk Nation 101

Crazy Horse 103

Chief Seattle 105

Cree Indian Prophecy 107

Iroquois Constitution 109

Cochise 111

Teedyuscung 113

Geronimo 115

Chief Keokuk 117

Great Spirit Prayer 119

Native American Diversity - Photos by Edward S. Curtis 120

ABOUT LITTLE HAWK 207

Biographical Sketch 209

Book: Learning Little Hawk's Way of Storytelling 212

Music: Little Hawk's Albums 214

Movie: REAWAKEN 216

Poem: Grandma, Grandpa 218

Good-Heart Tribe Contract 220

Little Hawk shares the message of love in his Grandmother's beadwork.
Still photo from the REAWAKEN movie. Watch it at ReawakenMovie.com.

"Best Guest Speaker to date."

PepsiCo Inclusion Council

Little Hawk has delivered his unique message of
Diversity & Inclusion to organizations such as:

PEPSICO

THE WHITE HOUSE

VERIZON

SONY

AT&T

AVIVA

FEDERAL EXECUTIVE BOARD

US ARMY

US NAVY

US AIR FORCE

EQUAL EMPLOYMENT OPPORTUNITY COMMISSION

FOREWORD
MULTICULTURAL INCLUSION:
THE THREAD THAT BINDS

I have known Little Hawk and Beverly for many years and they have always taught the timeless truth of having love and respect for all people, as well as respect for our Mother Earth. When we show kindness to one other, we are recognizing that we are all part of the same human family.

As Little Hawk says, "We are all related." It is this very simple message of inclusion and respect for all life (rather than separateness) that defines the essence of what Little Hawk and Beverly are all about. Compassion is their creed, which they have delivered to delighted audiences all over the globe.

As of this writing in October 2011, the world is full of chaos, yet it is more interconnected and multicultural than ever before in history. Through the technological advances of the Internet and the economic evolution of international finance, diverse populations and businesses are communicating with one another in greater numbers everyday. Global interdependence is a reality. We are literally connected by our computers, tablets, and cell phones.

Although many parts of the world, including the U.S., continue to be divided by nation, religion, race, gender, and class status, there is a much greater appreciation and awareness today for the benefits of working cooperatively to build healthier relations.

Strangely enough, it is the highly competitive field of the corporate workplace that has made the most substantial progress in this area. The many hard lessons learned since the civil rights movement of the 1960's reveal that a business grows stronger and more profitable as it practices greater Diversity and Inclusion in all its affairs. Diversity is an asset!

Nearly every major corporation in the 21st century has a human resources policy of Diversity and Inclusion that goes beyond the legal requirements of anti-discrimination and equal opportunities for employment. Executives and employees are faced with multicultural issues every day, both within the office and in the marketplace. Understanding and caring about customers, as well as fellow employees, is why companies are serious about their multicultural Diversity programs.

As further evidence, there are now official corporate Diversity and Inclusion departments that have fully developed executive career paths. Eighty percent of the Fortune 500 have a Diversity and Inclusion policy listed on their public web sites. Over 20 percent have an official top executive position called "Chief Diversity and Inclusion Officer" or "Director of Diversity."

IBM, one of the world's top global brands, has been a leader in Diversity and Inclusion for over a hundred years since it hired its first female employee, African-American employee, and handicapped employee in the early 1900's. In 2010, IBM's U.S. Diversity Recruiting Manager, Lisa Gable, told INSIGHT Into Diversity magazine:

"Diversity has always been a part of our fabric and what we believe helps bring innovation to the workplace. You need a workforce that mirrors your customer base."

Wall Street firm, Morgan Stanley describes their Diversity program as a competitive advantage on their website:

"The spirit of inclusion sharpens our competitive edge, fosters innovative thinking, and helps produce superior solutions for our clients."

These are not idle statements. The fact is Diversity and Inclusion are very Big Business.

In a recent publication, "Doing Business in a Multicultural World," the Director of the United Nations Alliance of Civilizations shared the following insight:

"Business is often at the forefront of creating space where people from different cultures meet and cooperate. The process of learning to work together is not always free of tension and mistakes are made. But overall, business has become a critical force in support of cultural understanding, building bridges between cultures and people by offering the prospect of economic opportunity."

It is this emphasis on cultural understanding and building bridges between cultures and people that makes Little Hawk's message so important for everyone to embrace.

As Little Hawk and Beverly share the wisdom of Diversity and Inclusion in this book, they remind each and every one of us that we are all connected by a common thread: The thread of unconditional love. And that thread of love comes from something greater than ourselves. Some call it God or a Higher Power. Little Hawk calls it the Great Spirit or the Great Holy. In any case, no matter what it is called, that thread of love is what we experience when we practice multicultural inclusion.

And that, my friends, is without any doubt, the common thread that binds us.

May you enjoy the following pages and be inspired by the Little Hawk message for many years to come.

—*John "Thunder Bear" Pritchard*

Little Hawk on tour in the Netherlands 2011.

INTRODUCTION

DIVERSITY LESSONS OF FIRST NATIONS PEOPLE

Not so long ago, Nature was respected with reverence and compassion. Stories were passed on from generation to generation. These tales told of animals singing, dancing, being happy, being sad, and speaking to each other about the lessons of life, which were easily learned and long remembered. All life was dependent on all life, humans included. In the Web of Life, we were and still are a part of ALL and ALL continues to be a part of us.

Storytelling is an important oral tradition for the First Nations People. Elders made the stories come alive. They became a part of the story, not just the teller of events. Through these oral traditions came entertaining stories and songs for all ages, to teach us we're connected to all other living things and how we can live IN A GOOD WAY.

The message was and is that all life is related and we must live in harmony with Nature and other people. This truth must be told to each generation so they, in turn, will teach their children the truth. Little Hawk hopes to leave people with the knowledge that they can make choices to live in harmony with one another and the environment.

For the children we were,
For the children still in us,
For the children now,
And for the children yet to come.

—Kenneth Little Hawk

SECTION 1:

IN THE WORDS OF LITTLE HAWK

THE LITTLE HAWK LOGO

THE MEDICINE WHEEL

The Medicine of knowledge, wisdom, and understanding is all around us, both in the seen and unseen world. All things being connected, the Medicine within each world keeps the continuity of the circle together, reproducing healthy results. Within the circle of the Earth, undiscovered medicines abound with treatments and cures for every illness. Knowing our Earth is our natural pharmacy is the key to health on all levels of life. Working to preserve it secures harmony and balance, now and in the future.

As Black Elk taught: "Birds make their nests in circles. We dance in circles. The circle stands for the Sun and Moon and all round things in the natural world. The circle is an endless creation, with endless connections to the present, all that went before and all that will come in the future."

Within the circle of the Medicine Wheel are four directions (north, east, south, and west), four elements (earth, water, air, and fire), four aspects of our own selves (physical, mental, emotional, and spiritual), and the four basic color combinations of the human beings. Because it is a circle, the Medicine Wheel represents the many cycles that appear in the natural world: The cycle of night and day, of the seasons, and of birth, life, and death.

The Little Hawk logo is a Medicine Wheel design. It was painted for me on my drum, in 1993, by a Hopi drummaker in Denver, Colorado, when I was performing in the award-winning play, "Black Elk Speaks."

The following are words from The Elder's Meditation of the Métis of Maine:

"The combination of heart and mind is very powerful. The Medicine Wheel teaches that two worlds exist—the seen and the unseen. The seen world is the physical and the unseen is the spiritual. Both of the worlds are necessary to discover true reality. The seen world is most easily seen by the male side. The unseen is most easily seen by the female side. The heart is the unseen and the mind is the seen. Blessed is the leader or person who has developed the heart and the mind. Truly, such a person is of tremendous value to the Creator and the people."

—Kenneth Little Hawk

WE ARE ALL RELATED

The rays of the sun affect us.
The moon's changing of the tide affects us.
The changing of the seasons affects us.
The sonic boom affects us.
War, disease, hunger, homelessness,
greed, and anger affects us.
Love, compassion, sharing, and caring affects us.
The movement of the planets, stars, asteroids,
comets, and meteors affects us.
The wind, rain, snow, heat, cold, humidity,
and dryness affects us.
The light, the dark, what we eat, feel, see,
hear, and touch affects us.
What is done to the air, water, and earth affects us.
What is done in Africa, Asia, Europe,
the Arctic, the Antarctica, and the Western
Hemisphere affects us physically, mentally,
emotionally, and spiritually.
Whether we can see it or not, it affects us.
If one part of the house is affected in some way,
so is the rest of the house.
We may live in another part of the house,
and our names may not be the same,
but our relationship remains the same.

We are all related.
What affects one, affects us all.
We are all related.

—Kenneth Little Hawk

BROTHER OF THE WIND

LET THE WINDS BLOW

Let the winds blow
Let the waters flow
Let the eagle fly
Let hate subside

Let the children live
Replace take with give
You're not better than
Any child, woman or man

How can you be
When you look at me
And not see yourself
In another human being
Who needs your help

Let the winds blow
Let the waters flow
Let the eagle fly
Let hate subside

We keep destroying the Earth
Our sacred mother
So how can we ever
Get along with each other

When we won't respect
The giver of life
All that's left
Is greed and strife

Let the winds blow
Let the waters flow
Let the eagle fly
Let hate subside

—Kenneth Little Hawk

WHERE WE USED TO RUN AND PLAY

Just the other day, I heard the children say,
"What happened to the field
where we used to run and play?
The trees are all gone—the grass is no more.

"Why, father, did they take it away?
This is where we used to run and play."
To make a place for cars to park—
that's why they took it away.
An empty answer to a broken, little heart.

"The chipmunks, birds, and squirrels—
Where did they all go?
Where will they live when it is cold
and the earth is deep in winter snow?
Where did they all go?

"Did they take them to another home?
All together—so they won't be alone?
To a place where they could run and play—
Since they took their homes away?
Why, mommy, did they take the field away?"

It's all been cut down, clean and bare.
A place to park cars was their only care.
Yes, they took the animals' homes away—
the trees, bushes, flowers,
and the place where the children used to
run and play.

I am sorry, children,
their heads are filled with dollar signs.
Their hearts are cold, not kind.
"Why did they take our place to play away?"
That's what I heard the children say,
standing here with them, just the other day.

Here where the children's laughter filled the air
Now trees, cut down, clean and bare.
The little stream where toy boats float,
no longer there.

"Please put it back as it was before.

"What happened to our trees—
the home of the birds and bees?
Around their trunks we'd run—
sit in the shade from the sun.
Where's our place of fun?
Why would they take it away?"
That's what I heard the children say,
just the other day.

The laughter that filled the air—
forever gone from there.
"Why would they take our field away?"
I heard the children say,
just the other day.

—Kenneth Little Hawk

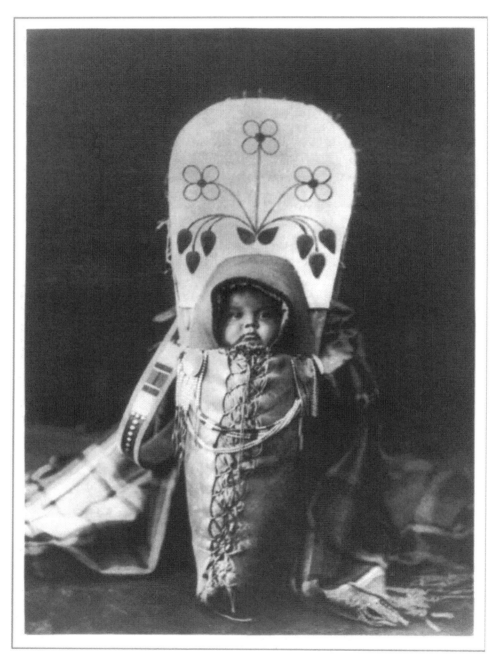

First Nations People always consider how the impact of their decisions
will affect the Seventh Generation to come.

THE SEVENTH GENERATION

If the truth were told 500 years ago
So much today
We would not have to say

So what comes from our mouth
To the young of our nation

So plain we see
Carries over to
The Seventh Generation

So what comes from our mouth
To the young of our nation

So plain we see
Has carried over to
The Seventh Generation

—Kenneth Little Hawk

SWEET SMELL OF PEACE

We have examples and lessons of the good way
All around us, every second of every day.

The animals, the air, the trees.
The wind, sun, moon, and stars.
The mountains, our pets, the rain, the clouds,
All of what we call Nature.

They all give without conditions.
They have not changed from the original plan
Given them by the Creator.
They have never varied from their paths.
To share, with each other, respect for all life.

Put the original plan back in action.
Put the glow of peace in your heart.

Let it shine!
Let it shine!
Let it shine!

Brighter than it ever has.

Hey! Ah-Ho!
Let it shine!
Let it shine!
Let it shine!

Brighter than it ever was.

—Kenneth Little Hawk

All birds, even those of the same species, are not alike, and it is the same with animals and with human beings. The reason Wakan Tanka does not make two birds, or animals, or human beings exactly alike is because each is placed here by WakanTanka to be an independent individuality and to rely upon itself.

—*Shooter, Teton Sioux*

THE BIRDS' SONG

We don't have to be
the same kind of bird
to have a beautiful song.

We can bring our songs together
so that our combined chorus
will resound to its fullest beauty.

—Kenneth Little Hawk

THE INDIAN ON THE LEDGE

An Elder once said to me, "The Earth is like a huge ball on a string being swung in a circle by the hand of *The Great Mystery*. The ball makes the sound of a slow heartbeat as it travels through space."

The soft wind sings a song of peace as it moves through the valleys and over the mountains. We can hear heaven's hum in our blood as it courses through our bodies, telling us our spirit is unlimited, whether on solid ground or on the ledge.

We are one with the Earth and one with the Earth's Spirit.

—Kenneth Little Hawk

SUNRISE ON THE MOUNTAINTOP

Fire and ice compliment each other and all life. Though one may seem to move out of the other's way, it is only showing a reverent respect for each other's abilities to give and renew life.

This shows us that nothing in Nature is diametrically opposed. Our relationship to one another depends on the spiritual reality of reverence for all that supports life's continuity.

Nature shows no favorites, but equally distributes to all, always giving, always renewing. What may seem opposite is, in reality, the same in its offerings.

—Kenneth Little Hawk

THE EAGLE FEATHER

The eagle feather is a symbol of:

- One who tells the truth
- One who can be trusted
- One who does not take credit
  for someone else's work
- One who is responsible for
  his or her own behavior

This is a good way for all to live together.

—Kenneth Little Hawk

AFTER THE RAIN

The Great Mystery's song is in all natural movement. When we listen with our hearts, we can hear the song the raindrops sing and see their dance of thanks to the hum of life.

We show reverence for *The Great Mystery's* creations through daily recognition of the songs and dances of rain, wind, fire, and all movement of the Earth.

—Kenneth Little Hawk

**Little Hawk in the dressing room of the Theater PePijn,
The Hague, Netherlands, 2011.**

THE GIFT

We are *containers* for the spirit.

Life is the gift that affirms the spirit.

The winged ones, insects, plant life, water life, and animal life are containers of the same gift of spirit.

To look for peace, sovereignty, success, love, happiness, and security outside our spirit is to hunt for an illusion—ever going away, never coming home.

—Kenneth Little Hawk

QUOTES FROM LITTLE HAWK

"TOO MUCH
WE USE OUR EYES,
AND SO LITTLE
DO WE SEE.

"WE ARE ALL RELATED.

"WHAT YOU DO,
ALSO AFFECTS ME."

—Kenneth Little Hawk

"HOW WOULD IT BE
IF YOU LOOKED AT ME
AS BROTHER?

"HOW WOULD IT BE
IF SHE LOOKED AT HER
AS SISTER?

"ELDERS AS GRANDMOTHER
AND GRANDFATHER?

"AND ALL OF THE CHILDREN
AS OUR OWN?"

—Kenneth Little Hawk
Lyrics from CD recording, *Relative*

"WE ARE A PART OF NATURE,
NOT APART FROM NATURE.

"LISTEN TO THE TREES,
THEY ARE TALKING TO US.

"TREES ARE THE
LUNGS OF THE EARTH."

—Kenneth Little Hawk

"LET US
FILL OUR HEARTS
WITH
PRAYERS OF PEACE
FOR
ALL PEOPLE."

—Kenneth Little Hawk

"WE CAN NO MORE
SEPARATE OURSELVES
FROM EACH OTHER
THAN HEAT
FROM THE FIRE."

—Kenneth Little Hawk

"WHETHER OUR **SHELTER**
IS MADE OF STICKS,
HIDES, **BARK,** CLAY OR MUD,
WE **ONLY** HAVE
THIS ONE **HOUSE**
– EARTH."

—Kenneth Little Hawk

"THERE IS
NO SEPARATION
BETWEEN CREATOR
AND CREATION."

—Kenneth Little Hawk

GRANDFATHER SAID,
"WE ARE ALL ONE PEOPLE
CALLED HUMAN BEINGS.
WE JUST LIVE
ON DIFFERENT PARTS
OF THE LAND."

—Kenneth Little Hawk

"IF WE HAVE FORGOTTEN
HOW TO TREAT
MOTHER EARTH,
HOW CAN WE
BE EXPECTED
TO REMEMBER
HOW TO TREAT
EACH OTHER?"

—Kenneth Little Hawk

Section 2:

Little Hawk's Stories of Respect and Compassion

ELDER AT THE GATHERING

The Elder asked, "How can we determine the hour of dawn, when night ends and day begins?"

Someone said, "It is when it is light enough that, at a distance, you can tell the difference between a wolf and a coyote."

Someone else said, "It's when it is light enough that, at a distance, you can tell the difference between a pine and a cedar."

The Elder said, "No, to both. It is when you look into the face of a human being and have enough light inside you to recognize him or her as brother and sister. Up until then it is night and darkness is still with us."

—As retold by Kenneth Little Hawk

TWO WOLVES

A Traditional Native Story

Grandfather and I were very close. He taught me to listen with my heart. One day when we were sitting together as we so often did, his head was down and he was quiet for a long time. Softly, I spoke to him, saying, "Grandfather, how are you feeling?"

He replied, "I am not feeling well, Little Hawk."

I asked, "What is it that is making you feel that way?"

Grandfather answered, "I feel like I have two wolves fighting in my heart. One wolf is mean and hateful, angry and bitter all the time. The other wolf is kind and caring, respectful and loving and peaceful all the time."

I could not hold back my words — they seemed to jump right out of my mouth. "Grandfather, Grandfather, which wolf will win the fight in your heart?"

Grandfather slowly raised his head, turned, and looked into my eyes. With the tiniest smile, he said, "The one that I feed."

—As retold by Kenneth Little Hawk

THE TALKING TREE

One day Grandfather came to me and said, "Ey, little one, do you know trees talk?"

"No, Grandfather, I did not know trees talk."

Then Grandfather said, "It is time that I show you how trees talk to us. Come, little one, we will walk to the ridge beyond the field where the line of trees begins. There we will sit and listen."

We sat and after a short time, Grandfather asked me if I heard the trees.

I answered, "No, I do not hear any words from the trees, Grandfather."

"You must listen with your heart," said Grandfather, "then you will see its goodness and you will hear it speak."

Grandfather continued, "I sat here yesterday and saw a man from Europe walking with his wife, his daughter, and his son. They stopped in front of that apple tree on the ridge, reached up and picked some apples off the branches, and began to eat the apples. With big smiles on their faces, they filled their stomachs and, after a while, picked up their bundles and continued on their way.

"Not long after that, a man from Africa stopped in front of that tree. He, his wife, and daughters began picking the fruit. And, just like the man from Europe and his family, the smiles on the faces of the family from Africa grew larger as they ate apples and their stomachs were filled with the sweet fruit. They rested before continuing on their journey.

"Then a family from China came along the path. The father and his wife and children stopped and picked fruit. Their words reached the branches as they thanked the tree and began to eat. The sweet juice from the apples ran down the sides of the little boy's mouth. They all laughed and picked up their bundles and walked on their way.

"Not long after the Chinese family was out of sight, a family from India noticed the tree. Speaking to his wife and daughters in their language, he pointed to the tree. The little girls began to do a dance because they were so happy to be handed the apples their mom and dad picked for them. As they sat eating the fruit, the picture of peace and love could be seen through their smiles. They rested with their backs against the tree. Then their parents picked up their bundles, the children stood up, and they continued on their way."

Then Grandfather asked me, "Do you hear now what the tree said?"

"No, Grandfather, I do not."

"Then I will tell you," said Grandfather. "The tree said we should be like the tree. The tree—with its branches full of fruit—did not say, 'You cannot have any of my apples because I don't like the language you speak.'

"The tree did not say, 'You cannot have any of my apples because I don't like the color of your skin.'

"The tree did not say, 'Because of the clothing you wear, you cannot have any of my apples.'

"The tree did not say, 'Because of your religion, you cannot have apples.'

"The tree shared what it had, teaching us generosity, teaching us equality. The tree did not show any racial hatred, religious bias, or selfishness. It shared its apples freely with all people. And we should share that which we individually and collectively have plenty of with all who are in need.

"The tree said, 'I live a long, long time, yet I do not stop sharing. Year after year, I continue to do the same for all those who come by. I give the people food, putting smiles on their faces, and encourage all the people to do the same.'"

Grandfather asked me, "Now, do you hear what the tree had to say to all who look and listen with their hearts?"

"Yes, Grandfather, now I hear the talking tree's message of goodness and sharing."

—Kenneth Little Hawk

The tree shared what it had, teaching us generosity, teaching us equality.

THE BIRDS HAD A CONTEST
A Traditional Native Story

A long time ago, before humans appeared on Earth, the birds decided to have a contest to see which bird could fly closest to the sun.

Birds were called from all over the land to gather at the place in the forest where the contest was to be held. There was much singing and chirping as the contestants waited.

The older birds were to be the judges. All of the birds were told to fly as high and as long as they could and then return to the starting place in the forest clearing.

One by one, owl, cardinal, flycatcher, sparrow, woodpecker, kingfisher, blue jay, hawk, and many others took their turn. When too tired to fly higher, each returned to the starting place in the forest.

The last of the birds to take its turn was Eagle. Higher and higher Eagle rose. He flew so high that he was just a little dot, way up in the sky. Knowing he had flown higher than all the other birds, Eagle turned and began his downward flight to the forest.

Just then, a tiny, little bird that had been hiding between the feathers of Eagle's wing, flew out and up above where Eagle had turned.

When both Eagle and the little bird stood before the judges, the little bird could no longer hold back its excitement. It shouted, "I won! I won! I won! All saw I flew higher than Eagle. I am the contest winner, I AM, I AM, I AM!"

The wise, old birds who were the judges said they needed to enter the Council Lodge to talk among themselves to name the winner. When they came out of the Council Lodge, they stood before Eagle, the little bird, and all those gathered at the forest clearing. They announced the Eagle was the winner. All around them the birds chirped and cheered.

"How can you say that?" shouted the little bird, who felt it was the winner.

The oldest bird began speaking, "All the other birds started from here. You started from the eagle's wing way up high. You rested while Eagle did all the work. You want to take credit for Eagle's accomplishment. You cheated—cheating is lying and you are not the true winner and you cannot be trusted."

All the birds cheered the eagle as the true and honest winner. "Hooray for the eagle! Hooray for the eagle!"

When the two-leggeds first appeared in North America, they were able to talk to and understand birds. The birds told them this story.

From that day to this day, the eagle feather has become a symbol of one who can be trusted, does not take credit for someone else's work, and is responsible for his or her own behavior. This is a good lesson of how everyone should live.

—As retold by Kenneth Little Hawk

Crow King, a Hunkpapa Sioux, was given an Eagle feather by Chief Sitting Bull for his bravery and leadership at the Battle of the Little Big Horn. Photographed by David F. Barry at Fort Buford, North Dakota, CA 1881.

Visit GoodHeartTribe.com and CareForTheEarth.org

THE GOOD-HEART TRIBE

From Kenneth Little Hawk's album "Care for the Earth"

There was a time, not too long ago, when forest animals looked about in alarm and saw the air was changing from clear and fresh to a gray-brown smog. As the wind blew, they could see the smog moving toward the valley. When it reached the valley, it became very hard for all to breathe.

The animals coughed and cried out, "The smog is getting thicker! Help! Help me!"

The forest animals quickly called a gathering, inviting all to attend. And so, all those who walked, crept, crawled, swam, and flew began to gather. Even the trees and the grass bent forward to hear. The rippling lake became quiet and the sun did its best to shine down through the smog.

"Look," Beaver shouted, smacking his large, flat tail on the ground. "The birds are leaving their nests as the thick, gray smog moves through the trees. It is hard for the bird families to breathe."

All around him, the birds began to cough. "Chirp! Cough! Chirp!"

Thunder Bear spoke next, saying that when he was a little cub, his Grandfather, Dancing Bear, told him a story. Dancing Bear had said, "Some day the forest animals will see the air become smoky and change color. Then it will be hard to see the forest around us and our eyes will sting and fill with tears. We will find it hard to breathe and each breath will make us sick. When this happens, our forest medicine will not help us."

Grandfather Dancing Bear had said, "Trees are the lungs for all living things on Earth. Trees help clean the air, too. If the trees stop breathing, we will stop breathing."

Grandfather had added, "As long as trees are plentiful and healthy, we, too, will be healthy. Our friends, the trees, provide homes for animals. They give us food. They regulate temperature and they hold the soil together. Many animals cannot survive without trees. And trees are such fun to climb!"

At this, Beaver shouted, "My family and I gnaw down trees to make our homes. Should we stop doing this?" He coughed and gasped for air.

A wise Elder, Grandfather Little Hawk swooped in, landing just in time to hear Beaver's worries. "Oh, no," said Little Hawk. "When you build your homes, you do not take many trees. You never take more trees than you need and those fallen trees make a dam for water. This gives our forest beautiful, natural lakes and ponds.

"And when summer's heat becomes too much, your dam has stored up plenty of water for all the animals, birds, fish, and insects. And, if it doesn't rain, the plants still have water to drink. Oh, no, you are not hurting! You are helping. We thank you for your dams, Beaver."

Grandfather Little Hawk hopped up on a tree stump and spoke again. "You can see the air is changing. It is causing us to cough! See this little, green blade of grass? It is now sick. The grass, trees, vines, berries, fruit, nuts, soil, and water will become sicker with each passing day. The two-leggeds' poisons are making Mother Earth and everything around it sick."

The Chipmunk, seated between the Spider and the Butterfly, was next to raise her little voice in fear. Although Chipmunk was young, everyone knew she was alert and quite smart, indeed. All attending the gathering moved closer so they wouldn't miss even one word.

"All our forest medicine is being poisoned, too! But I know what we can do. Send those two-leggeds back to where they came from so they cannot do any more harm to us and Mother Earth. But wait! Wait! The people of the First Nations do not hurt the Earth. They can stay! Let's send the others back!"

"Yes!" Thunder Bear snarled. "We of the Forest were here first. We were doing just fine. None of us ever even thought of making the Earth sick."

Then all the other animals started to chatter and call out, "Send them back! Send them back! Send them back to where they came from!"

Thunder Bear rose up on his hind legs, pawing the air, and growled. "GRRRRRRRRR!!!!!! Where did they come from? One morning we just woke up and found them walking around. Stomping through our forest! Is there any of us that knows where they came from?"

A hush fell over the animals. Each thought and thought, but none could answer the question.

Finally, Grandfather Elk rose and spoke softly. "When I was small, it was said that they came from the mist, as it moves onto the land, just before daybreak. You know…that mist that hovers over the great water as it is slowly pushed by the wind."

Then very wise, very thoughtful Owl fluttered her wings and hooted, "It has been said that they came from a mixture of water and soil."

Moose frowned at this for she had heard the two-leggeds fell through a hole in the sky and landed in the mountains, then rolled down to the forest floor, and arrived feeling very angry!

Grandfather Little Hawk bowed his head. "It does not matter where these new two-leggeds came from. They are here now and we must decide how to stop them from making air hard to breathe. We must have a ceremony and ask for answers."

All the animals, insects, birds, and even the trees, grass, and lake began calling to the Great Spirit.

"Teach us! Show us the way! Teach us and show us the way!"

The sun struggled to be seen through the smog and tried to light their way. And, as the wind moved through the tops of the trees, they heard a great voice echoing across the hills and water. The Great Spirit spoke.

"Each of you must continue to live in a good way. You must continue to set an example for others."

"Ah, that is our answer," whispered Turtle.

Wolf stepped forward, his yellow eyes gleaming. "Yes, we must teach the two-leggeds by our own example. Whenever we wolves leave our den to look for food, we never leave our little ones unattended. We always assign responsibility to a teenage wolf. This builds confidence in decision making, while protecting our cubs from straying. This teaches authority and respect to the teen."

Off in the woods, the other wolves howled in agreement.

Then Uncle Duck waddled up. His feathers were all fluffed out as a sign he had been chosen to speak for both ducks and geese. He quacked and honked to get their attention. And then he spoke:

"We can teach them. When we fly in V-formation, everyone gets the chance to lead. The leader at the front of the V must break through the air. This makes the path easier for those flying behind. And the ones behind the leader voice their encouragement. They say, 'You are doing a good job! Thank you for making it easier for us to follow you!'"

The other ducks and geese quacked or honked in agreement so Uncle Duck paused, making sure he still had everyone's attention before continuing.

"When our flight leader gets tired, he or she goes to the back. Then another one of us takes the head wind. And we never abandon those in trouble. If one of us is too sick or ill to continue, another of us goes down with the weak one to stay with him until he is better."

The sly Fox sat up and looked at them with narrowed eyes. "When my family lived by the ocean, we moved to higher ground many hours before ocean storms came to the land. We were able to keep out of harm's way."

Then Elk and Ram spoke as one. "We, who live in the forest and mountains, know days before a volcano erupts. So, when you see us moving away from the mountain, you should move, too."

They heard little squeaks and it was Mother Mouse who pushed forward to speak next.

"When you see us come above ground bringing our families and all of our relatives, take notice! We know an earthquake is coming! Then you must leave that place as quickly as you can!"

A sudden hush fell over the animals, as the Great Spirit's voice echoed through the forest.

"These are wonderful examples of how to treat your own families, and how to treat each other. But teaching these examples to the new two-leggeds will not keep them from making more smog. It will not stop more bad air from being put into your lungs, and into the trees, and the water, and grass. These examples will not keep them from blocking out the sun with their smog.

"They have been seeing all these fine examples of your daily behavior for a long time. Still they choose to harm us and our Mother —and their Mother, too—the Earth. They do not listen. How now will you teach them good behavior? How will you show them what not to do? How will you get them to listen?"

All those at the gathering remained silent. Each was thinking of the best way to answer the Great Spirit.

Finally, three Ravens fluttered into the center of the circle, each cawing out at once.

"I know!"

"I know!"

"I know!"

The first Raven cried out, "We must teach them that the forest and its creatures are not enemies to be harmed. They must not take more from our forests, rivers, lakes, and land than they need to sustain themselves. They must learn that each living thing on this Earth is connected. We must teach them that each one of them, each animal, each tree, each blade of grass, each drop of water, each bit of blue sky, and golden ray of the sunlight is important to everything else. They must learn that everything on our Earth must live together in a good way."

The second Raven flapped his wings excitedly. "And the two-leggeds must be taught not to waste. Or leave trash behind. Or set fires in the woods. I mean, it takes so very long for trees to grow back. It is not good to be careless."

The third Raven stepped forward looking at all of the animals and shouted, "Yes! The people of the First Nations knew that they must be the caretakers of the Earth and of this forest. These new two-leggeds must learn this lesson, too! They must learn to be responsible. If they are not going to contribute to Mother Earth's well being, they should not damage her. Or cause her to be sick. We all depend on each other to keep the Earth healthy."

Again the Great Spirit's voice echoed across the water, hills, and trees.

"But what if the two-leggeds still do not care? What will you do then, my beautiful Ravens?"

The three Ravens took a moment to confer. Then the largest one looked up proudly. "Oh, Great Spirit! It is still not too late. Even if they will not choose to walk the good path, their children may still learn to become the caretakers of the Earth! The children can be made aware of the destruction taking place all around them. They are young enough to learn the consequences that their choices will have! I hope that they will choose to pass on a healthy world to their own children, and their children's children, for the next Seven Generations yet to come."

At this, all the animals nodded wisely. Then the smallest Raven recalled an old Cree proverb.

"When the Earth is sick, the animals will start to disappear. When this happens, the Warriors of the Rainbow will come to save them."

Mother Mouse turned and looked at the sky saying, "Great Spirit, can it be that these children may yet grow to be those Warriors of the Rainbow?"

The Great Spirit spoke again.

"Yes, we are all part of this Earth. The responsibility as caretakers should not always fall on the people of the First Nations or our forest's creatures. The newcomers have many, many children. If their children choose to become Rainbow Warriors, the ancient Cree prophecy will have come to pass. Yes, I am most satisfied with this answer."

The Great Spirit was pleased and, so, the animals at the gathering were satisfied. Then Thunder Bear rose up again and growled loudly enough for all to hear.

"GRRRRRRRR! The Great Spirit has found that these children are the ones who will listen. And we agree that they are the ones who will help us save our homes and take care of Mother Earth. Now we must form a new tribe for them and it shall be called the Good-Heart Tribe. Go now to all the children and invite them to be members of the Good-Heart Tribe! GRRRRRRRR!"

At that moment, the smog on the mountain began to clear. And the animals at the conference each took a deep breath. The wind rustled through the trees whispering, "In a good way...in a good way." The lake began rippling again and two little fish jumped right out of the water, singing out, "In a good way!"

And all the animals shouted with joy, "Hooray for the children! They will join our Good-Heart Tribe! They will keep the water clean and save us! We will teach them that everywhere in Nature, there are lessons to help guide our behavior in a good way.

As the fish splashed back into the lake, the sky cleared, and the sun could be seen again, smiling at its reflection in the lake.

And so all of those at the gathering went off in all four directions looking for the Children of the Rainbow to invite them to join the Good-Heart Tribe.

And this is a story that shows we are all a part of Nature—not apart from Nature. All children who are listening to this story know this message is for them:

You are the Children of the Rainbow and the time has come for you to join the Good-Heart Tribe. You can save the animals' homes. You can take care of Mother Earth. Yes, you are the caretakers of the forest. You are the Children of the Rainbow.

Kenneth Little Hawk telling a story to Wambli Cochise Martinez,
Lakota and Apache, seven years old, June 2010.
Photographer, Tony "Silent Thunder" Austin, Massasoit.

THANK YOU, GRANDFATHER

A Traditional Native Story

The little boy asked his Grandfather,
"Grandfather, Grandfather, teach me to be an Indian."

Grandfather said, "Come with me down to the pond."

When they reached the pond, Grandfather said, "Pick up that stick over there, put it down into the bottom of the pond, and stir it around very fast, very fast."

As the little boy did this, the rocks at the bottom of the pond became dislodged; the plants wrapped around the stick and were jerked out of the muddy water.

The fish and the other water animals started darting away to the other side of the pond.

Grandfather said, "Now come sit next to me and let us watch."

As the water cleared, Grandfather said, "Now put it back the way it was."

The little boy said, "Grandfather, I can not do that."

Grandfather replied, "Now you know what it is to be a human being. You are learning what it is to be a human being."

"Thank you, Grandfather," the little boy replied,
"Thank you, Grandfather.
Thank you, Grandfather.
Thank you, Grandfather."

—As retold by Kenneth Little Hawk

SECTION 3:

NATIVE AMERICAN WISDOM

WORDS OF PEACE
In many Native Languages

Awige, "Peace" (Algonquian)

Achwangundowagan, "Lasting peace" (Delaware/Lenape)

Aquene, Ahque, "Peace, end of hostilities" (Mashantucket Pequot}

Her'kv, "Peace" (Muscogee Creek)

Wetaskiwin, "Hills of peace" (Alberta Cree)

Aquene, "Peace" (Southern New England, Algonquian)

Waunakee, "We have peace" (Great Lakes Algonquian)

Langundowi Litehewagan, "Thoughts of peace" (Delaware)

Langundowagan, "Peace and amity" (Delaware)

Wulangundowagan, "Peace" (Delaware)

Wulangundik, "Keep peace" (Delaware)

Wulatschimoisin, "To treat about peace" (Delaware)

Malu, "Peace" (Hawaiian)

Laule'a, "Peaceful, happy time" (Hawaiian)

Techqua Ikachi, "Blending with the land and celebrating life" (Hopi)

Onen, "Peace be with you" (Iroquois)

Orenda, "Peaceful spirit" (Iroquois)

Wowalj'wa, "Peace" (Lakota)

Aquewopuan wock, "Hold your peace" (Mashantucket Pequot)

Hozhqqji, "Blessingway" (Navajo)

Mitakuye Oyasin, "With all things we are related" (Sioux)

Aquene-ut, "Place of peace" (Wampanoag)

SACRED WAY PRAYER
Based on an Ojibwe Prayer

O' Great Spirit,
look at our brokenness.

We know that in all creation
only the human family has strayed from the
Sacred Way.

We know that we are the ones
who are divided
and we are the ones
who must come back together
to walk in the Sacred Way.

Great Holy, Sacred One,
teach us love, compassion, and honor that we
may heal the Earth
and heal each other.

Chief Joseph (1871-1904)

EQUAL JUSTICE

If the white man wants to live in peace with the Indian,
he can live in peace...

Treat all men alike. Give them all the same law.
Give them all an even chance to live and grow.
All men were made by the same Great Spirit Chief.

They are all brothers. The Earth is the mother of all people,
and all people should have equal rights upon it....

Let me be a free man, free to travel, free to stop,
free to work, free to trade, where I choose my own teachers,
free to follow the religion of my fathers,
free to think and talk and act for myself,
and I will obey every law, or submit to the penalty.

—Heinmot Tooyalaket (Chief Joseph),
Nez Perce Leader (1871-1904)

A TRADITIONAL CHINOOK BLESSING

We call upon the waters that rim the Earth, horizon to horizon, that flow in our rivers and streams, that fall upon our gardens and fields, and we ask that they
Teach us and show us the way.

We call upon the land which grows our food, the nurturing soil, the fertile fields, the abundant gardens, and we ask that they
Teach us and show us the way.

We call upon the forests, the great trees reaching strongly to the sky with their roots in the earth and the heavens in their branches, the fir and the pine and the cedar, and we ask them to
Teach us and show us the way.

We call upon the creatures of the fields and forests and the seas, our brothers and sisters, the wolves and deer, the eagles and doves, the great whales and dolphins, the beautiful orca and salmon who share our home, and we ask them to
Teach us and show us the way.

We call upon those who have lived on this Earth, our ancestors and friends, who dreamed the best for future generations, and upon whose lives our lives are built, and, with thanksgiving, we call upon them to
Teach us and show us the way.

And lastly we call upon all that we hold most sacred, the presence and power of the Great Spirit of love and truth which flows through the Universe, to be with us to
Teach us and show us the way.

Chief Sitting Bull (1831-1890)

"EACH MAN IS GOOD
IN THE SIGHT
OF THE GREAT SPIRIT.
IT IS NOT NECESSARY
FOR EAGLES
TO BE CROWS."

—Chief Sitting Bull, Teton Sioux (1831-1890)

"THERE ARE **MANY** THINGS
TO BE SHARED
WITH THE **FOUR COLORS**
OF **HUMANITY**
IN **OUR** COMMON DESTINY
AS **ONE** WITH OUR
MOTHER THE **EARTH**.
IT IS **THIS** SHARING
THAT MUST BE **CONSIDERED**
WITH GREAT CARE
BY THE **ELDERS**
AND THE **MEDICINE** PEOPLE
WHO CARRY
THE **SACRED** TRUSTS,
SO THAT **NO** HARM
MAY **COME** TO PEOPLE
THROUGH **IGNORANCE**
AND MISUSE
OF THESE POWERFUL **FORCES**."

—Resolution of the Fifth Annual Meetings
of the Traditional Elders Circle, 1980

"WE ALL COME
FROM THE SAME ROOT,
BUT THE LEAVES
ARE ALL DIFFERENT."

–John Fire Lame Deer, Lakota

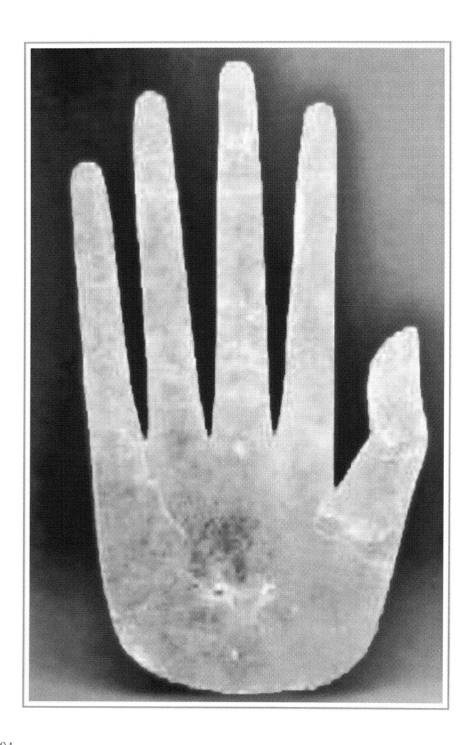

"EACH **CREATURE**
HAS A **MEDICINE**,

SO THERE ARE

MANY MEDICINES."

—Wallace Black Elk,
Holy Man of Oglala, Lakota (1921-2004)

Mourning Dove was a Native American author best known for her 1927 novel Cogewea the Half-Blood: A Depiction of the Great Montana Cattle Range, which tells the story of Cogewea, a mixed-blood ranch woman on the Flathead Indian Reservation. The novel is one of the first written by a Native American woman and one of few early Native American works with a female central character. She is also known for Coyote Stories (1933), a collection of Native American folklore (using her term).

Mourning Dove is the English translation of her Indian name, Hum-isha-ma; her English name was Christal Quintasket. She was born in 1888 near Bonners Ferry, Idaho, to a Colville mother and a half-Okanagan, half-Irish father. She died on August 8, 1936.

"...EVERYTHING ON THE EARTH
HAS A PURPOSE,
EVERY DISEASE
AN HERB TO CURE IT,
AND EVERY PERSON
A MISSION.
THIS IS THE INDIAN THEORY
OF EXISTENCE."

—Mourning Dove, Salish (1888-1936)

Oren Lyons, Jr. was born in 1930 and raised in the culture and practices of the Iroquois on the Seneca and Onondaga reservations in Upstate New York.

Lyons served in the United States Army. He received an athletic scholarships to Syracuse University, where he was awarded the Orange Key for his academic and athletic accomplishments. where he graduated from the College of Fine Arts in 1958. A lifelong lacrosse player, Oren was an All-American at Syracuse, where the Syracuse Orange men's lacrosse went undefeated during his graduating year. After graduation, Lyons played for several teams, including the New York Lacrosse Club (1959-1965), the New Jersey Lacrosse Club (1966-1970), and the Onondaga Athletic Club (1970-1972).

Upon leaving Syracuse, Lyons pursued a career in commercial art in New York City, becoming the art and planning director of Norcross Greeting Cards. Outside of work, Lyons exhibited his own paintings during this time. In 1970, Lyons returned to Onondaga to be closer to his cultural heritage. In recognition of his contributions over many years as a teacher of undergraduate and graduate students in the University at Buffalo, Dr. Lyons is listed as SUNY Distinguished Service Professor and Professor Emeritus of American Studies in the UB College of Arts and Sciences.

"WE FORGET
SO WE CONSIDER
OURSELVES SUPERIOR.
BUT WE ARE, AFTER ALL,
A MERE PART
OF THE CREATION.
WE STAND SOMEWHERE
BETWEEN THE MOUNTAIN
AND THE ANT."

—Chief Oren Lyons, Faithkeeper of the Turtle Clan,
Onondaga Nation of the Hau de no sau nee (Born 1930)

The **Nuxalk Nation** (Nuxalk; *Nuxálk*; pronounced [nuxálk], with the 'x' like German *ach*), also referred to as the **Bella Coola** or **Bellacoola**, are an Indigenous First Nation in Canada, living in the area in and around Bella Coola, British Columbia. Their language is also called Nuxalk.

The name *Bella Coola*, often used in academic writing, is not preferred by the Nuxálk; it is thought to be either a derivation of the neighbouring coastal Heiltsuk people's name for the Nuxálk, *bɫxʷlá* (rendered *plxwlaq's* in Nuxalk orthography), meaning "stranger".

The Nuxalk peoples, known collectively as Nuxalkmc, were four tribes (the Kimsquit from Dean Channel, the Tallheo/Talio from South Bentinck, the Stuic (Stuie) from Tweedsmuir Park, and the Kwalhna/Kwatna from King Island) who gathered in their current Bella Coola Valley, settling together based on cultural and linguistic similarities. Not everyone settled within the current Nuxalk Nation, and as such the Nuxalk share many family ties with their neighbours and beyond, most extensively with the Heiltsuk.

The Nuxalk Nation is a member of the Oweekeno-Kitasoo-Nuxalk Tribal Council, and until March 2008 was a member of the Unrepresented Nations and Peoples' Organization.

"WE MUST PROTECT THE FORESTS FOR OUR CHILDREN, GRANDCHILDREN, AND CHILDREN YET TO BE BORN. WE MUST PROTECT THE FORESTS FOR THOSE WHO CAN'T SPEAK FOR THEMSELVES SUCH AS THE BIRDS, ANIMALS, FISH, AND TREES."

—Qwatsinas, Hereditary Chief Edward Moody, Nuxalk Nation

"WE DO NOT INHERIT
MOTHER EARTH
FROM OUR ANCESTORS.
WE BORROW HER
FROM OUR CHILDREN."

—Crazy Horse, Tashunca-uitco (1840-1877)

Crazy Horse was a Native American war leader of the Oglala Lakota. He took up arms against the U.S. Federal government to fight against encroachments on the territories and way of life of the Lakota people, including leading a war party at the Battle of the Little Bighorn in June 1876. After surrendering to U.S. troops under General Crook in 1877, Crazy Horse was fatally wounded by a military guard while allegedly resisting imprisonment at Camp Robinson in present-day Nebraska. He ranks among the most notable and iconic of Native American tribal members and has been honored by the U.S. Postal Service with a 13¢ Great Americans series postage stamp.

Chief Seattle (1780-1866)

"ALL THINGS SHARE
THE SAME BREATH—
THE BEAST, THE TREE, THE MAN.
THE AIR SHARES ITS SPIRIT
WITH ALL THE LIFE
IT SUPPORTS."

—Chief Seattle led the Duwamish and Suquamish (1780s-1866)

Cree Camp 1871

The Cree are one of the largest groups of First Nations/Native Americans in North America, with 200,000 members living in Canada. In Canada, the major proportion of Cree live north and west of Lake Superior, in Ontario, Manitoba, Saskatchewan, Alberta, and the Northwest Territories, although 15,000 live in eastern Quebec.

In the United States, this Algonquian-speaking people lived historically from Lake Superior westward. Today, they live mostly in Montana, where they share a reservation with the Ojibwe (Chippewa).

"Only AFTER the last TREE
has been CUT down;
Only after the last FISH
has been CAUGHT;
Only after the last RIVER
has been POISONED;
ONLY then
will you REALIZE
that MONEY
CANNOT be eaten."

—Cree Indian Prophesy

The Iroquois Constitution of the Five Nations provided a significant inspiration to Benjamin Franklin, James Madison and other framers of the United States Constitution. Franklin circulated copies of the proceedings of the 1744 Treaty of Lancaster among his fellow colonists; at the close of this document, the Iroquois leaders offer to impart instruction in their democratic methods of government to the English. John Rutledge of South Carolina, delegate to the Constitutional Convention, is said to have read lengthy tracts of Iroquoian law to the other framers, beginning with the words "We, the people, to form a union, to establish peace, equity, and order..." In October 1988, the U.S. Congress passed Concurrent Resolution 331 to recognize the influence of the Iroquois Constitution upon the U.S. Constitution and Bill of Rights.

"IN ALL YOUR DELIBERATIONS
IN THE COUNCIL, IN YOUR EFFORTS AT
LAWMAKING,
IN ALL YOUR OFFICIAL ACTS,
SELF-INTEREST
SHALL BE CAST INTO OBLIVION.

"CAST NOT AWAY THE WARNINGS
OF ANY OTHERS IF THEY SHOULD CHIDE YOU
FOR ANY ERROR OR WRONG
YOU MAY DO, BUT RETURN
TO THE WAY OF THE GREAT LAW,
WHICH IS JUST AND RIGHT.
"LOOK AND LISTEN FOR THE WELFARE OF
THE WHOLE PEOPLE AND HAVE ALWAYS IN
VIEW NOT ONLY THE PRESENT,
BUT ALSO THE COMING GENERATIONS,
EVEN THOSE WHOSE FACES ARE YET
BENEATH THE SURFACE OF THE EARTH
—THE UNBORN OF THE FUTURE NATION."

—Iroquois Constitution of the Five Nations

Cochise (or "Cheis") was one of the most famous Apache leaders (along with Geronimo) to resist intrusions by Americans during the 19th century. He was described as a large man (for the time), with a muscular frame, classical features, and long, black hair which he wore in traditional Apache style. He was about 5'10" tall and weighed about 175 lbs. In his own language, his name "Cheis" meant "having the quality or strength of oak."

"YOU MUST **SPEAK** STRAIGHT
SO THAT YOUR **WORDS**
MAY **GO** AS **SUNLIGHT**
INTO OUR HEARTS."

—Chief Cochise, Chiricahua Apache (1823-1874)

Teedyuscung (1700–1763) was known as *King of the Delawares*. He worked to establish a permanent Lenape (Delaware) home in eastern Pennsylvania in the Lehigh, Susquehanna and Delaware River valleys. Teedyuscung participated in the Treaty of Easton, which resulted in the loss of any Lenape claims to all lands in Pennsylvania. Following the treaty the Lenape were forced to live under the control of the Iroquois in the Wyoming Valley near modern day Wilkes-Barre.

Teedyuscung was murdered by arsonists on April 19, 1763 as he reportedly lay asleep as his cabin burned around him. This marked the beginning of the end of the Lenape presence in Pennsylvania. Teedyuscung's son Chief Bull conducted a raid on the Wyoming Valley that was part of a greater Indian uprising, which resulted in the Lenape being forced to move west of the Appalachian Mountains by the Royal Proclamation of 1763.

"...LET **NOTHING**
DISCOURAGE YOU
TILL **YOU**

HAVE ENTIRELY
FINISHED
WHAT YOU
HAVE **BEGUN**."

—Teedyuscung, Delaware (Died 1763)

Geronimo

On March 6, 1858, a company of 400 Mexican soldiers attacked Geronimo's camp while the men were in town trading. Among those killed were Geronimo's wife, his children, and his mother. It was the Mexicans who named him *Geronimo*. This appellation stemmed from a battle in which, ignoring a deadly hail of bullets, he repeatedly attacked Mexican soldiers with a knife, causing them to utter appeals to Saint Jerome ("Jeronimo!"). The name stuck.

"I cannot THINK
THAT WE ARE USELESS
OR GOD WOULD NOT
HAVE CREATED US.
WE ARE ALL
THE CHILDREN
OF ONE GOD.
THE SUN,
THE DARKNESS,
THE WINDS
ARE ALL LISTENING
TO WHAT WE
HAVE TO SAY."

—Geronimo, Chiricahua Apache (birth date unknown-1909)

Chief Keokuk of the Sauk Tribe (1767-1848)

Keokuk was a chief of the Sauk or Sac tribe in central North America noted for his policy of cooperation with the U.S. government which led to conflict with Black Hawk, who led part of their band into the Black Hawk War.[1] Keokuk County, Iowa and the town of Keokuk, Iowa, where he is buried, are named for him.

"Do NOT
KILL TREES,
DO NOT
DISTURB THE WATER
AND THE RIVERS.
DO NOT
POACH THE BOWELS
OF OUR EARTH.
OTHERWISE,
THE RIVERS
AND THE TREES
WILL CRY."

—Chief Keokuk, Sauk Tribe (1767-1848)

GREAT SPIRIT PRAYER

Oh, Great Holy, whose voice we hear in the wind. Hear us!
Let us listen with our hearts so we may hear the groans of Mother Earth who feeds us, cleans us, clothes us, gives us drink, houses us, and gives us medicine—as she has given to our ancestors.

Oh, Great Holy, whose breath gives life to all the world. Hear us!
Let us listen with our hearts that we may hear the cries of the children who have no food, no homes, no clothing, no clean water, no medicine, and no mother or father to comfort them in their final hours.

Oh, Great Holy, we are small and weak. Let us listen with our hearts, that we may hear the moans of anguish of the mothers and fathers, who watch their babies waste away, as their little spirits leave with each tear that rolls down their faces.

Oh, Great Holy, we need your strength and wisdom. Let us listen with our hearts, that we may hear the sorrow in the eyes of the elders who are disrespected by all those who have shut themselves from the wisdom, knowledge and understanding that the elders have gathered on their paths of right.

Oh, Great Holy, let us listen with our hearts to the voices of the ancestors, that we may hear them say, "Let not our lives that came before you, be lives that had no meaning for those yet to be born, for it is from us you came."

Oh, Great Holy, let us listen with our hearts so we may hear the cries of all life, the world over. We are not separate. We are all connected. We are all related. We are the voices of our ancestors, and the guides for future generations.

Oh, Great Holy, look at our brokenness. We know that in all creation, only the human family has strayed from the Sacred Way. We are the ones who are divided and we are the ones who must come together to walk in the Sacred Way that we may heal the Earth and heal each other.

—Author Unknown

NATIVE AMERICAN DIVERSITY

Edward S. Curtis visited more than than 80 tribes in the early 1900's and took more than 40,000 photographs. The following images are courtesy of the U. S. Library of Congress.

POMO TRIBE

TSAWATENOK TRIBE

Hidatsa Tribe

X1704-05

SAN ILDEFONSO TRIBE

WISHRAM TRIBE

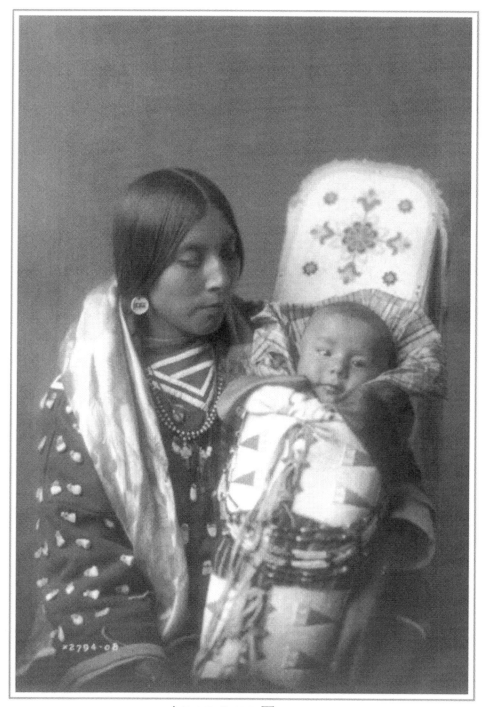

Aparoke Tribe

HUPA TRIBE

YANKTONAI TRIBE

Navajo Tribe

PIEGAN   UTE   APACHE

COMANCHE   BRULE SIOUX   OGLALA SIOUX

Nunivak Tribe

NUNIVAK TRIBE

NAVAJO TRIBE

MANDAN TRIBE

Zuni Tribe

PIMA TRIBE

NAVAJO TRIBE

Hupa Tribe

WISHRAM TRIBE

NOATAK TRIBE

ARIKARA TRIBE

CHEYENNE TRIBE

Sioux Tribe

SAN ILDEFONSO TRIBE

SIOUX TRIBE

WISHRAM TRIBE

APSAROKE TRIBE

San Ildefonso Tribe

OGLALA TRIBE

NOATAK TRIBE

Hidatsa Tribe

KLAMATH TRIBE

ZUNI TRIBE

JEMEZ TRIBE

Acoma Tribe

MOJAVE TRIBE

NUNIVAK TRIBE

APSAROKE TRIBE

NUNIVAK TRIBE

CROW TRIBE

NEZ PERCE TRIBE

NEZ PERCE TRIBE

WISHRAM TRIBE

PIEGAN TRIBE

Navajo Tribe

QUILLIUTE TRIBE

APACHE TRIBE

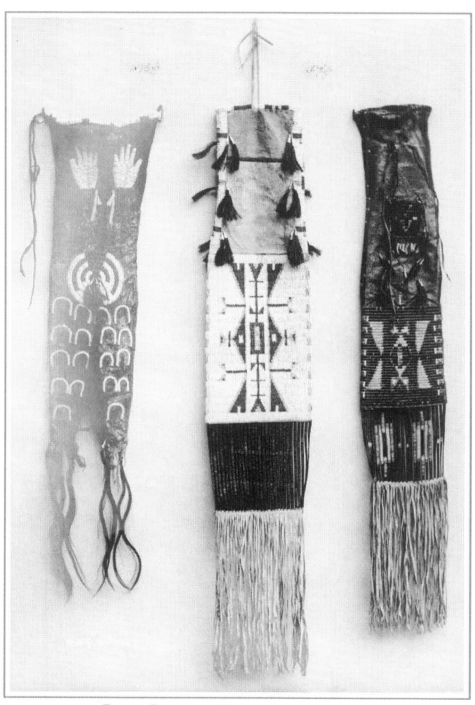

PIPE BAGS - TRIBE UNKOWN

OGLALA TRIBE

HIDATSA TRIBE

APSAROKE TRIBE

CROW TRIBE

NAMBE TRIBE

PIEGAN TRIBE

CREE TRIBE

NUNIVAK TRIBE

First Nations people created shelters from natural elements in their environment that suited their lifestyles and climates. Some shelters were made of clay, mud, rocks, grasses, hides, bark, branches, straw, and ice.

INUIT HUT

WICHITA TRIBE

APACHE TRIBE

Cahuilla Tribe

NAVAJO TRIBE

Hupa Sweat House

HOPI TRIBE

HOPI TRIBE

HOPI TRIBE

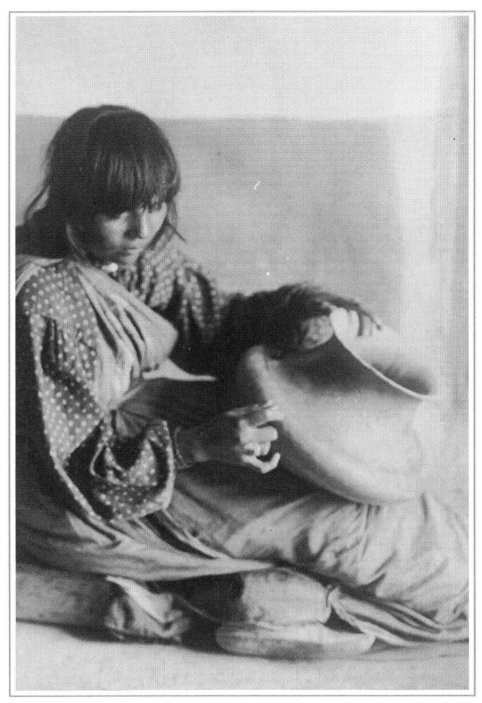

Santa Clara Tribe

ZUNI TRIBE

MARICOPA TRIBE

KAHATIKI TRIBE

MARICOPA TRIBE

KOTZEBUE TRIBE

ABOUT
LITTLE HAWK

BIOGRAPHICAL SKETCH

Kenneth Little Hawk is a descendant of the Mi'kmaq and Mohawk tribes. He is a spellbinding storyteller, keynote speaker, recording artist, flutist, singer, dancer, and actor, who has traveled throughout the world, teaching people from all walks of life the ways of his ancient culture. When Little Hawk combines the wisdom of his ancestors with his talents, his public performances are described as "a museum exhibit come alive."

Little Hawk shares his wisdom so we may mend the global hoop that encompasses all life. He says he does this, "For the children we were, for the children still in us, for our own children now, and for the children yet to come." Whenever he is invited to speak, his message is always the same: "We can make choices to live in harmony with one another and with our environment."

Touring throughout America over the past 27 years, Little Hawk has performed for over three million people at many distinguished locations including Lincoln Center and the Museum of Natural History in New York, and the Kennedy Center in Washington. In 1998, he was a guest of the President and performed at the White House for a special screening of the PBS film, "Lewis & Clark." Our government has referred to Little Hawk as a national treasure.

Little Hawk has been nominated twice for Best Storyteller of the Year by the *Native American Music Awards* for WIND, SUN AND STARS and IN A GOOD WAY. In reviewing WIND, SUN AND STARS, FANFARE magazine reported, "The stories are fascinating and the presentation avoids condescension. It is polished, but not slick. This CD rings true."

The review for IN A GOOD WAY reported, "Excellent storytelling! Very animated and sound effects of the animals and nature made the stories come alive."

Little Hawk's voice and authentic flute music can be heard in such award-winning PBS films as THE WEST and LEWIS AND CLARK produced by the acclaimed director, Ken Burns. A documentary, THREE WISE MEN, was filmed in Australia in 2006 to preserve Little Hawk's teachings. In the 2010 inspirational movie, REAWAKEN, Little Hawk shares his stories and wisdom about sharing your good heart.

Little Hawk's powerful presence and dignity has lent itself to stage roles in BLACK ELK SPEAKS, INDIANS, THIS LAND IS WHOSE LAND, and THE INHERITANCE. His film credits include THE WEST, LEWIS AND CLARK, LAND OF THE EAGLE, PETTY CRIMES, and CAMPFIRE STORIES. He is a member of the Screen Actors' Guild and Actors' Equity.

Little Hawk with his Grandmother's beadwork.

"What Little Hawk has to teach is exactly what America has to learn."
Pete Seeger, Folk Singer

Learning Little Hawk's Way of Storytelling

by
Kenneth Little Hawk
and Beverly Miller
as taught to
Frank Domenico Cipriani

NEW BOOK ...

LEARNING LITTLE HAWK'S
WAY OF STORYTELLING

Little Hawk shares his oral storytelling traditions as he was taught by his grandparents. The practical skills illustrated through the telling of both traditional and contemporary stories are easily embraced. They come from the universal appeal of respect and compassion.

By following the life of a man destined to become a storyteller, the reader, too, gains many of the skills needed to captivate as well as educate others.

So many good books on this subject stress that storytelling is an excellent teaching tool; yet no other book actually uses teaching stories to teach storytelling. Like all of Little Hawk's stories, it can also be enjoyed by children, while teaching them the art of storytelling.

Another unique aspect of this book is that the teacher-character is based on Little Hawk himself.

Published by Findhorn Press — findhornpress.com
ISBN 978-1-844089-536-0
Published June 1, 2011
Available at Amazon.com & Barnes & Noble.

IN A VERY REAL WAY

Kenneth Little Hawk

THE GREAT MYSTERY

Kenneth Little Hawk

IN A GOOD WAY

Kenneth Little Hawk

FIRST LIGHT by SINH•TALA

Kenneth Little Hawk, Greg Reeves
& John Pritchard

THE TALKING TREE

Kenneth Little Hawk
& Thunder Bear

RELATIVE

Kenneth Little Hawk
& Ema

amazon.com®

NEW MUSIC ...

Albums are available at KennethLittleHawk.com, iTunes, or Amazon.com.

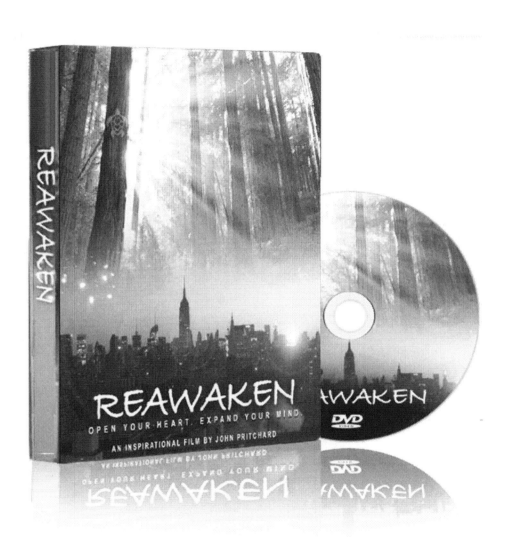

New Movie: REAWAKEN

Be inspired by Native American Storyteller, Kenneth Little Hawk, who shares his grandparents' timeless wisdom.

- Increase your love and respect for all life
- Share your compassion and good feelings with the world
- Open your heart and listen with your spirit, not your ears

REAWAKEN is an inspirational movie about opening your heart and expanding your mind. American filmmaker, John Pritchard encourages you to tap into your own inner potential by increasing your creativity, intuition, and laughter. The film features Native American storyteller, Kenneth Little Hawk, and five other champions of the human spirit: Grammy Award-winning musician, Fred Lipsius; Writer/Editor, Deborah Brown; Boat builder/Entrepreneur, Gene Carletta; Energy Medicine/ Health expert, Susan Stone; and Master Woodworking instructor/ Guitarist, Jim Markham.

REAWAKEN promotes optimism, compassion, and hopefulness. The movie is presented in five multi-dimensional parts with additional Bonus Footage:

PART 1: SPIRITUAL GENIUS
PART 2: LAUGHTER
PART 3: CREATIVITY
PART 4: INTUITION
PART 5: UNCONDITIONAL LOVE

REAWAKEN will not only help you recognize the spiritual genius within you, but also encourages you to be more helpful to your family, friends, co-workers, and the world at large. Is there anything more important? Open your heart. Expand your mind. Love and laughter connects us all!

VISIT REAWAKENMOVIE.COM

GRANDMA, GRANDPA

Grandma, Grandpa, you taught me never to say goodbye
Thank you for keeping our spirit alive
Grandma, Grandpa, your spirit alive in every way
Guiding me everyday I pray

Grandma, Grandpa, the ancestors you spoke of
with reverent smile, respect and love
Grandma, Grandpa, you shared their wisdom everyday
prayers they taught you in the same way

Grandma, Grandpa, with heart open my eyes do see
The things you always wished for me
Grandma, Grandpa, now I share in the same way
the lessons you taught me every day

Grandma, Grandpa, what others could not feel or see
now so plain as real could be
Grandma, Grandpa, giving thanks each day you were my guide
Your spirit in me rests deep inside

—Kenneth Little Hawk

WWW.GOODHEARTTRIBE.COM

KENNETH LITTLE HAWK'S
GOOD-HEART TRIBE

I WILL TREAT ALL PEOPLE WITH RESPECT.

I WILL CARE AND SHARE.

I WILL BE KIND TO ANIMALS.

I WILL LIVE IN HARMONY WITH NATURE.

I WILL GIVE MY HEART
LOTS OF CHANCES TO BE GOOD.

_____   _____
NAME   DATE

Printed in Great Britain
by Amazon